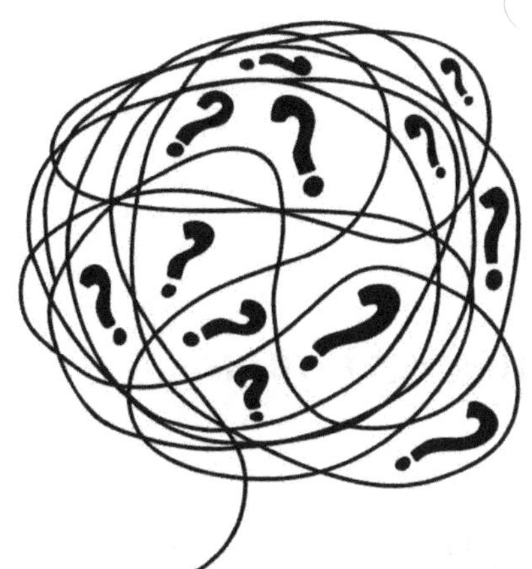

UNDERSTANDING HARD QUESTIONS

I Need Answers!

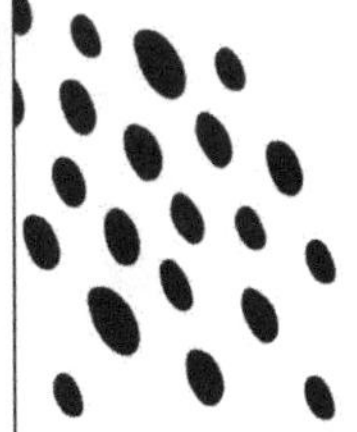

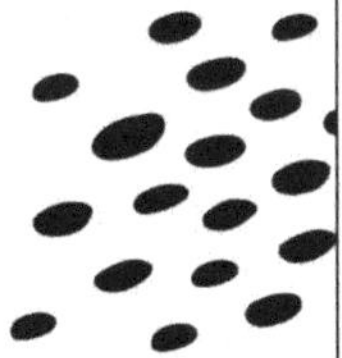

Janine McNally

UNDERSTANDING HARD QUESTIONS
I Need Answers.

ISBN - Paperback: 979-8-9896732-8-5
Second Edition: December 2025
Printed in the United States of America.

Janine McNally, Th. M., D. Min.
Panama City, FL 32401
Janine@EquippingFireflies.com

Dear Parents

Preteens are in a HUGE time of transition, undergoing massive changes as they prepare for adulthood. They ask serious questions, and we need answers, or they will look elsewhere.

This book answers fifty-six of the most common questions from an age-appropriate biblical perspective.

- Who created God?
- Does God speak to people?
- Will God stop loving me if I keep sinning?
- How did Jesus perform miracles?
- Why do people get sick and die?
- Why did my parents get divorced?
- Can Christians lose their salvation?
- How can God forgive murderers?
- Why is sex outside of marriage wrong?
- Are there more than two genders?
- Can I be sure that I will go to heaven?
  And more!

Parents and grandparents can participate in this discipleship process by encouraging your child or grandchild, answering their questions and stepping in to help when needed.

Remember:

- Pray for your child that they will grow to know Jesus more each day.
- Don't expect your children to be perfect. Even though they may be saved, they are still sinners.
- Help them look up Bible verses and write answers in their books.

The extent to which your child will apply these lessons depends largely relies on the support and encouragement you provide as a parent.

We are praying for you.

> *"These commandments that I give you today are to be on your hearts.* ***Impress them on your children.*** *Talk about them* ***when you sit at home, when you walk along the road, when you lie down, and when you get up."***
> Deuteronomy 6:6-7 [NIV].

Understanding Hard Questions

Table of Contents

Questions About God

1. What is God Like?

The Bible tells us a LOT about God.

Most importantly, the Bible teaches that there is only ONE God.
But the Bible also teaches us that God is THREE People in ONE.

The technical term for this is the "Trinity."

1. God the Father.
2. God the Son [Jesus].
3. God the Holy Spirit.

Each of them is God but is also one unique Person with a specific job.

This isn't easy to understand, but it's really important. There is no easy way to explain it, but it's a bit like the Celtic Trinity Knot. The design has three loops, but when you trace the loop pattern, there is no beginning or end.

It's all one connected line!
God the Father, God the Son, and God the Spirit are not three Gods.

The circle in the knot pattern reminds us that God is ONE God and also THREE Persons.

As we answer questions about God, try to keep this in your mind.
It will help explain some of the questions.

So, what is God like?

Here are some of the things that we know about God.

- God is perfect (holy) (Psalm 18:30; Deuteronomy 32:4).
- God is immortal (eternal) (1 Timothy 6:16).
- God is Infinite (Psalm 147:5).
- God is unchanging (Psalm 55:19).
- God is all-powerful (Psalm 115:3; Isaiah 55:11; Jeremiah 32:17).
- God is all-knowing (1 John 3:20; Romans 11:3).
- God is invisible (John 1:18; Colossians 1:15).

- God is impartial (He has no favorites) (Romans 2:11-12; Colossians 3:25).

There are many more verses in the Bible that talk about God. You can find out more by reading a little each day!

2. What Does God Look Like?

We don't know what God looks like.

The Bible tells us that God is invisible.

> *"The Son [Jesus] is* ***the image of the invisible God****."*
> Colossians 1:15 (NIV).

> *"Now to the King eternal, immortal,* ***invisible****,*
> *the only God, be honor and glory for ever and ever."*
> 1 Timothy 1:17 (NIV).

The Bible also says that no person has ever seen God.

> ***"No one has ever seen God***
> *but the one and only Son [Jesus]."*
> John 1:18 (NIV).

But there are times when God shows Himself in a different form, like when He appeared to Moses in a burning bush.

> *"Do not come any closer," God said. "Take off your sandals,*
> *for the place where you are standing is holy ground."*
> *Then He said, "I am the God of your father, the God of*
> *Abraham, the God of Isaac, and the God of Jacob." At this,*
> ***Moses hid his face,***
> ***because he was afraid to look at God****."*
> Exodus 3:5-6 (NIV).

God showed Himself as fire in a burning bush.

When Moses realized that God was speaking to him, he hid his face. He was afraid to look at God.

Later, God made it clear that you cannot look at God and live.

> *"But," He said, "You cannot see My face,*
> ***for no one may see Me and live."***
> Exodus 33:20 (NIV).

So, bottom line, no one knows what God looks like. But one day, we will see Him face-to-face! (Revelation 22:3-4).

3. Who Created God?

You might wonder, "Who created God?" Where did He come from?

The Bible tells us that no one created God.
God was never created.
God has always just "been."

God has always existed. He created everything! He is the beginning of everything.

Nothing existed before God because He created all that exists.

> *"I am the Alpha and the Omega,* ***the Beginning and the End,****" says the Lord God. "I am the God* ***who is****, and* ***who was****, and* ***who will come****. I am the Mighty One."*
> Revelation 1:8 (NIV).

It's hard to understand that someone was just there.

Things have to be made by someone, right?
They can't just exist on their own, can they?

Everything has a beginning. Doesn't it?
It couldn't just "appear."

But God was.

It's not easy to understand, but it shows us that God is powerful and will always be there to take care of us!

4. When Was God Born?

God has always existed. He created everything! He is the beginning of everything.

> ***"Before the mountains were born or You brought forth the whole world,***
> *from everlasting to everlasting, You are God."*
> Psalm 90:2 (NIV).

God was never born, nor will He get old. He has no beginning or end.

> *"**In the beginning**, Lord, You laid the foundations of the earth, and the heavens are the work of Your hands. **They will perish,***
> ***but You remain**... they will be changed.*
> *But You remain the same,*
> *and **Your years will never end**."*
> Hebrews 1:10-12 (NIV).

But God the Son, Jesus, was born and lived approximately thirty-three years before He died on the cross.

Our calendar is based on the approximate time when He was born.

The year tells us how long ago Jesus was born. So, if it is 2024, Jesus was born just over two thousand years ago.

5. Does God Have a Body?

God the Father is a spirit and does not have a human body.

But if you read the Bible carefully, you will read that God is described as having eyes (Daniel 9:18; Amos 9:3), ears (1 Peter 3:12), hands (Isaiah 5:25), and feet (Isaiah 63:3).

It tells us that:

- God smells food (Genesis 8:21).
- God eats and drinks (Judges 9:13).
- God speaks (Genesis 1:3; Leviticus 4:1).
- God listens (Exodus 16:12).
- God even whistles (Isaiah 7:18).

It doesn't mean that He has actual body parts.

It's the Bible teaching us about God using language that we understand.

Jesus, God the Son, came to earth as a baby and grew up, just like we do. So, for those 33 years, Jesus had a human body.

- He was born like us.
- He became a man and walked on earth, just like we do.
- He lived on earth, and then He died.
- He received a new body when He went back to heaven.

Jesus' human body was transformed into a new heavenly body after He was raised back to life. He appeared to the disciples in this new body (Matthew 17:1-13; Mark 9:2-13; Luke 9:28-36).

His face shone like the sun, and His clothes became dazzling white with bright rays of light.

His disciples still recognized Jesus, and He stayed with them for forty days before returning to heaven.

God, the Holy Spirit, is a "spirit," so He doesn't have a physical body.

6. What is God's Name?

God has many names and titles in the Bible
Here are some of them.

- El Shaddai (Lord God Almighty) Genesis 17:1
- El Elyon (The Most High God) Gen 14:18
- Adonai (Lord, Master) Exodus 4:10
- Yahweh (Lord, Jehovah) Genesis 2:4
- Jehovah Nissi (The Lord My Banner) Exodus 17:15
- Jehovah-Raah (The Lord My Shepherd) Psalm 23:1
- Jehovah Rapha (The Lord That Heals) Exodus 15:26
- Jehovah Jireh (The Lord Will Provide) Genesis 22:14
- Jehovah Shalom (The Lord Is Peace) Judges 6:24

There are MANY more!
Each name tells us what God is like.

7. How Old is God?

We already talked about how no one created God. God has always just "been."

He was there at the beginning and will be there at the end.

That's because God has no beginning or end.

> *"In the beginning, Lord,*
> *You laid the foundations of the earth, and the heavens are the work of Your hands. They will perish, but You remain... they will be changed. But You remain the same, and* ***Your years will never end.****"*
> Hebrews 1:10-12 (NIV).

God was never born, nor will He get old.

So, God has no age! We get old, but God doesn't.

8. Where Does God Live?

God's home is in Heaven.

> *"But You rule* ***from Your throne*** *as the Holy One."*
> Psalm 22:3 (NIRV).

In Old Testament times, God dwelt in the temple.

> *"Our parents were unfaithful; they did evil in the eyes of the Lord our God and forsook Him. They turned their faces away from* ***the Lord's dwelling place****."*
> 2 Chronicles 29:6 (NIV).

The Lord's "dwelling place" was the temple. People came to the temple to worship God and make sacrifices.

The Bible says that God now lives with His people. When Jesus was born, He lived on earth.

> *"The Word became a human being.*
> ***He made His home with us****."*
> John 1:14 (NIRV).

When Jesus came back to life, He left earth and returned to heaven. God sent His Holy Spirit to live in us to help us become more like Him.

> *"Don't you know that* ***your bodies are temples of the Holy Spirit? The Spirit is in you.****"*
> 1 Corinthians 6:19 (NIRV).

The Holy Spirit comes to live within us when we trust in Jesus.

> *"You are being made into a house* ***where God lives through His Spirit.****"*
> Ephesians 2:22 (NIRV).

9. Does God Ever Sleep?

God does not have a physical body like us, so He doesn't need to eat or sleep.

> *"He won't let your foot slip. He who watches over you won't get tired. In fact, He who watches over Israel* ***won't get tired or go to sleep.****"*
> Psalm 121:3-4 (NIRV).

The Bible talks about Him resting after He created the world.

But it wasn't because He was tired.

Z Z Z Z Z Z Z Z

In fact, God is always working.

> *"Jesus said to them,*
> ***"My Father is always doing His work.***
> *He is working right up to this day. I am working, too."*
> John 5:17 (NIRV).

God set an example to teach us that it is OK to stop working and rest.

I NEED ANSWERS?

10. Does God Speak to People?

Yes, God does speak to people.

Some people in the Bible heard the audible voice of God, like Samuel.

> *"The Lord came and stood there.*
> *He called out, just as He had done the other times.*
> *He said, "Samuel! Samuel!"*
> *Then Samuel replied, "**Speak. I'm listening**."*
> 1 Samuel 3:10 (NIRV).

He speaks through people.

> *"In the past, God spoke to our people*
> ***through the prophets.** He spoke at many times.*
> *He spoke in different ways."*
> Hebrews 1:1 (NIRV).

God sometimes speaks to people in dreams.

> *"And afterward, I will pour out My Spirit on all people.*
> *Your sons and daughters will prophesy, your old men*
> *will **dream dreams**, your young men will see visions."*
> Joel 2:28 (NIV).

He can even speak in a whisper.

> *"After the earthquake came a fire, but the Lord was not in the fire. And after the fire came* ***a gentle whisper****."*
> 1 Kings 19:12 (NIV).

He speaks through events in our lives.

> *"He [God]* ***marked out their appointed times in history*** *and the boundaries of their lands. God did this so that they would seek Him."*
> Acts 17:26-27 (NIV).

God works in our lives so that we will follow Him.

> *"Before I was afflicted, I went astray, but now I obey Your word."*
> Psalm 119:67 (NIV).

God also speaks through creation.

> *"****The heavens declare the glory of God****; the skies proclaim the work of His hands. Day after day, they pour forth speech; night after night, they reveal knowledge."*
> Psalm 19:1-2 (NIV).

Most often, though, God speaks to us through His Word, the Bible.

> *"**All Scripture is God-breathed** and is useful for teaching, rebuking, correcting and training in righteousness."*
> 2 Timothy 3:16-17 (NIV).

11. Does God Cry?

The Bible talks about God having different emotions.

- He laughs (Psalm 2:4)
- He gets angry (1 Chronicles 13:10)
- He hates (Leviticus 20:23)
- He takes revenge (Isaiah 1:24).
- He gets jealous (Exodus 20:5).

When Jesus came to earth as a man, the Bible tells us He was sad and cried.

He cried when Lazarus died:

> *"Where have you put him? [Lazarus]" He asked. "Come and see, Lord," they replied.* ***Jesus wept.****"*
> John 11:35 (NIRV).

Jesus cried when the people of Jerusalem rejected God.

> *"As He [Jesus] approached Jerusalem and saw the city,* ***He wept over it.****"*
> Luke 19:41 (NIV).

God does not shed real tears, but He does feel sad when

people are hurting.

> *"The Lord is close to those whose hearts have been broken. He saves those whose spirits have been crushed."*
> Psalm 34:18 (NIRV).

He is sad when people disobey Him.

> *"How often they refused to obey Him in the desert!*
> *How often they **caused Him sorrow***
> *in that dry and empty land."*
> Psalm 78:40 (NIRV).

And He is sad when people don't believe Him.

> *"**The Lord was very sad** that He had made human beings on the earth. His heart was filled with pain."*
> Genesis 6:6 (NIRV).

12. Does God Have a Mom and Dad?

Since God the Father was never born, He does not have a mom or dad like us.

But when Jesus came to earth as a baby, He had a whole family.

- He had a Mom - Mary.
- He had brothers and sisters.

Jesus' brothers are mentioned in several Bible verses (Matthew 12:46; Mark 3:31; Luke 8:19; John 7:1-10; Acts 1:14).

The Bible tells us that Jesus had four brothers: James, Joseph, Simon, and Judas (Matthew 13:55).

The Bible also tells us that Jesus had sisters, but we are not told how many (Matthew 13:56).

Most Christians believe that Jesus was not married, so He had no wife. If He did, we are not told in the Bible.

13. Does God Have Friends?

God is made up of three People:

1. God the Father.
2. God the Son.
3. God the Holy Spirit.

Because of this, He is never alone.
However, God created people so that we could get to know Him.

> *"We do it so you can share life together with us.*
> ***And we share life with the Father and with His Son, Jesus Christ."***
> 1 John 1:3 (NIRV).

He desperately wants to share life with us and call us "friends."

> *"I no longer call you servants*
> *because a servant does not know his master's business.*
> *Instead,* ***I have called you friends."***
> John 15:15 (NIV).

14. What Does God Do With All of His Time?

We are not told what God does with all of His time. But the Bible tells us a few things.

- God rests (Genesis 2:3), but He does not get tired.
- God planted a garden (Genesis 2:8).
- God walks (Genesis 3:8), and He sits (Psalm 2:4).
- God closed the door of Noah's Ark (Genesis 7:16).

God doesn't live with human time. For Him, 1000 years is like a day.

> *"But do not forget this one thing, dear friends: With the Lord,* ***a day is like a thousand years, and a thousand years are like a day.****"*
> 2 Peter 3:8 (NIV).

So, God is not sitting around twiddling His thumbs, waiting for things to happen. It's another one of those things that are difficult for us, as humans, to understand.

15. How Did God Create the World?

God is so powerful; all He had to do was say the word!

> ***"The Lord merely spoke,***
> ***and the heavens were created.***
> *He breathed the word, and all the stars were born.*
> *He assigned the sea its boundaries and locked the oceans in vast reservoirs. Let the whole world fear the Lord, and let everyone stand in awe of Him.*
> ***For when He spoke, the world began!***
> ***It appeared at His command."***
> Psalm 33:6-9 (NIV).

God spoke a word, and everything was created.

Just. Like. That!

16. Why Did God Create the World?

God created the world and everything in it because He wanted to.

He wanted a place for people to live.

He wanted people to be part of His family and created the world for us to live in and enjoy.

"In the beginning, God created the heavens and the earth."
Genesis 1:1 (NIV).

His creation shows us God's power.

"Then God looked over all that He had made.
It was excellent in every way."
Genesis 1:31 (NIV).

17. Why Did God Make People?

God created the world because He wanted to.
God made people also because He wanted to.
God made us like Himself so that we could know Him.

He wanted a relationship with us, so He created us in His image.

> *"Then God said, "Let Us make man **in Our image**, after our likeness…" So, God created man in His own image; in the image of God, He created them male and female."*
> Genesis 1:26-27 (NIV).

People are the only part of God's creation that can have a relationship with Him.

18. How Can God Be Everywhere?

God is in all places at all times.
He is "omnipresent."

The word "omnipresent" is two Latin words put together:
"Omni" = "All" or "every."
"Present" = "To be present."
So, "omnipresent" means that God is "all-present."
He is everywhere.

God can be everywhere because God is a Spirit.
He lives in Heaven, but He is with us here on Earth.

> *"There is no one like the Lord our God.* ***He lives in the heights above, but He bends down to see the heavens and the earth.***" Psalm 113:5-6 (NIRV).

So, God can be everywhere at all times – because He is GOD!

19. Does God Know the Future?

Do you ever wonder if God knows what is going to happen in the future?

The answer is YES!

God knows everything – yesterday, today, and tomorrow. He knows what has already happened in the past and what will happen in the future.

He is Omniscient.
"Omniscient" is another big word made up of two Latin words. ("omni + scient").

"Omni" means "All."
"Scientia" is Latin for "knowledge."

What does the word "scient" sound like to you?
Yes – In English, we get the word "science."

So, God has "all knowledge."

He knows the past, present, and future! We can trust Him!

I NEED ANSWERS?

20. If God Can Do Anything, Why Doesn't He Stop Sin?

God is omnipotent. I bet you can figure out what this word means without any help.

"Omni" = "All"
"Potent" = "To have great power."

The Bible teaches us that God is all-powerful. He can do anything that He wants to do. Nothing or nobody is stronger than God.

> *"Ah, Sovereign Lord, You have made the heavens and the earth by* ***Your great power*** *and outstretched arm.* ***Nothing is too hard for You.****"*
> Jeremiah 32:17 (NIV).

- He could stop sin.
- He could stop war and violence.
- He could stop pain and suffering.

So why doesn't He?

God gave people a free will and a choice.

God didn't want robots.
He wants people to choose Him.

Unfortunately, we chose sin.

But one day, God will put an end to sin.

- There will be peace.
- God will take away all pain and suffering.
- He will wipe away all tears.

> *"**He [God] will wipe away every tear** from their eyes. There will be **no more death or sadness**. There will be **no more crying or pain.** Things are no longer the way they used to be."*
> Revelation 21:4 (NIRV).

Now that's something to look forward to!

21. Why Does God Love People?

The Bible tells us that GOD IS LOVE.
It is His very nature to love.

It's who He is.
He can't help Himself.

- God doesn't love us because we're good or nice people.
- God doesn't love us because we love Him.
- God doesn't love us less when we disobey and sin.

Nothing we do could make God love us more.
Nothing we do could make God love us less.

> *"But **here is how God has shown His love for us**. While we were still sinners, Christ died for us."*
> Romans 5:8 (NIRV).

He doesn't love us because of anything we do or don't do.
He just LOVES US!

22. Will God Stop Loving Me if I Keep Sinning?

God's love is UNCONDITIONAL.
That means that He will love us no matter what.

Conditional love is when we say things like.

- I'll be your friend as long as you are nice to me.
- I'll help you as long as you say, "Please."
- If you are mean to me, I won't be your friend anymore.

We place conditions on our love.

But God's love is UN-CONDITIONAL.
That means He has NO conditions.
He loves us just the way we are.

He will NEVER stop loving us!

23. Can God Forgive the Same Sin Over and Over?

Yes, He can! And He does!

Doing the right thing isn't easy.

Even the apostle Paul said that he wanted to do the right things but found himself doing the wrong things again and again. This is what he said.

> *"We know that the law is holy.* ***But I am not.***
> *I have been sold to be* ***a slave of sin****. I don't understand what I do. I don't do what I want to do.*
> *Instead,* ***I do what I hate to do."***
> Romans 7:14-15 (NIRV).

Sin comes naturally.

You never have to teach a toddler how to stomp their feet.
You never have to teach a child how to tell a lie.
It comes naturally.
We will always sin because it's in our nature.
We will often find ourselves committing the same sins again and again.

But God loves us more than we can understand.
He knows that we face struggles and temptations.

> *"But God is faithful and fair. If we admit that we have sinned,* ***He will forgive us our sins. He will forgive every wrong thing we have done."***
> 1 John 1:9 (NIRV).

When we admit that we were wrong, He promises forgiveness.

As we get to know God more, we will become more like Him.
Hopefully, we will sin less.

> *"Let the one who is evil* ***stop doing evil things****. And let him* ***quit thinking evil thoughts****. Let him turn to the Lord. The Lord will show him His tender love.* ***Let him turn to our God****. He is always ready to forgive."*
> Isaiah 55:7 (NIRV).

Questions About Jesus

1. Is Jesus God?

Yes!

Jesus is God.

One of His names is the "Son of God", but He is fully God.

Read these verses and fill in the blanks.

> *"We also know that the Son of God has come...*
> *And we belong to the true God by belonging to* ***His Son, Jesus Christ. He is the true God and eternal life."***
> 1 John 5:20 (NIV).

Jesus is the T __ __ __ God.

> ***"The Son [Jesus] is the exact likeness of God,***
> *who can't be seen."*
> Colossians 1:15 (NIRV).

Jesus is the "E __ __ __ __ likeness" of God.

Another name for Jesus is the "Word."

Before anything else existed, there was God's Son.
He was the Word, and He was with God.

> *"In the beginning, the Word was already there. The Word was with God, and **the Word was God**."*
> John 1:1 (NIRV).

The Word (Jesus) was G __ __.

So yes, Jesus is God.

2. How Did Jesus Perform Miracles?

Jesus was able to do miracles because He is God.

He is all-powerful.

Jesus did many miracles. The Bible tells us about some of them.

For example:

- Jesus walked on water (Matthew 14:25-30).
- Jesus calmed a storm (Matthew 8:23-27).
- Jesus turned water into wine (John 2:1-11).
- Jesus healed the sick (Matthew 15:19-20).
- Jesus cast out demons (Mark 1:23-28).
- Jesus raised people from the dead (Matthew 9:23–25).

Jesus did many miracles and each one demonstrated His power.

> *"Jesus left there. He walked along the Sea of Galilee. Then He went up on a mountainside and sat down. Large crowds came to Him. They brought blind people and those who could not walk. They also brought disabled people, those who could not speak, and many others. They laid them at His feet, and* ***He healed them.****"*
> Matthew 15:19-20 (NIV).

What are some of things that Jesus healed that are mentioned in these verses?

____

____

____

Jesus was able to perform all of these miracles because He is God.

3. Why Did Jesus Have to Die?

The perfect Son of God did not deserve to die.

He lived a perfect life.

Jesus suffered a horrible death:

- The soldiers beat Him
- They put a crown of thorns on His head
- People mocked and spit on Him
- They pierced His hands and feet with nails.
- He was hung on a wooden cross and left to die.

If Jesus didn't deserve to die, then why did He?

Jesus died for us.

He died so that we wouldn't have to.

See, the Bible says that we are all sinners.

Read this verse and fill in the blanks.

> *"**For all have sinned** and fall short of the glory of God."*
> Romans 3:23 (NIV).

How many people have sinned? A __ __.

Do you know what sin is?

Sin is anything that goes against God's perfect standard.

- Have you ever told a lie?
- Have you ever stolen something?
- Have you ever been mean to your brother or sister?
- Have you ever disobeyed your parent or teacher?

Perhaps you didn't answer every question with a "yes," but even if you have done only one thing wrong, it means you're a "sinner."

God's standard is 100% perfect.
Not 50%, 90% or even 99%.

You might think that you are a "good" person, but God's standard is 100%.

Just like one drop of poison would ruin a glass of pure water, just one sin makes us sinners.

Just one sin ruins perfection.

And there is a penalty for that sin.

Read this verse.

> *"For **the WAGES of sin is death**, but the gift of God is eternal life, through Jesus Christ our Lord."*
> Romans 6:23 (NIV).

Wages are what you earn. It's payment for your work and time.

The Bible says that the penalty for sin is D __ __ __ __.

But there is good news.

Read this verse.

> *"But God demonstrates His own love for us in this: While we were still sinners, **Christ died for us**."*
> Romans 5:8 (NIV).

What did Jesus Christ do for us?

He D __ __ __ for us.

Couldn't God have saved sinners some other way?

No. Jesus dying for us is the only way.

He took our place and died so that we wouldn't have to.

It was the ONLY way for us to be saved.

If He didn't die, then we would have to.

4. Why Is Jesus' Resurrection Important?

After Jesus died, He was buried in a grave.

Three days later, something amazing happened.

Jesus came back to life.
He was resurrected.

"Resurrected" means to come back to life after you die.

God raised Jesus from the dead.

The Bible says:

> *"Christ died for our sins, just as Scripture said He would. He was buried.* ***He was raised from the dead*** *on the third day."*
> 1 Corinthians 15:3–4 (NIRV).

Jesus' friends found His tomb empty.
Later, they saw Him and even touched Him.

For forty days, Jesus stayed on earth, proving that He really was alive.

Then, Jesus went back to heaven to be with God.

So, why is Jesus' resurrection important?
Why couldn't Jesus pay for sin by dying on the cross and then staying dead?

1. The resurrection shows that Jesus is the Son of God, with the power to come back to life.

> *"The reason My Father loves Me is that I give up My life. But I will take it back again.* ***No one takes it from Me.*** *I give it up Myself. I have the authority to give it up. And I have the authority to take it back again."*
> John 10:17-18 (NIRV).

Jesus G __ __ __ up His life and then He T __ __ __ it back again.

He has the "authority" to do that because He is God.

2. If Jesus had stayed dead, He would still be under the punishment and power of sin [death].

But Jesus Christ proved that He had victory over sin and death by coming back to life.

Read these verses.

> *"**Death, where is the victory you thought you had**? Death, where is your sting?" The sting of death is sin... He gives us the victory because of what our Lord Jesus Christ has done."*
> 1 Corinthians 15:55-57 (NIRV).

Have you ever been stung by a bee?
It's not fun, is it?

This verse tells us that death has a S __ __ __ __.
But Jesus took it away when He rose again.

Now we don't have to be afraid of dying.

3. The resurrection shows that God will give believers a new body after they die.

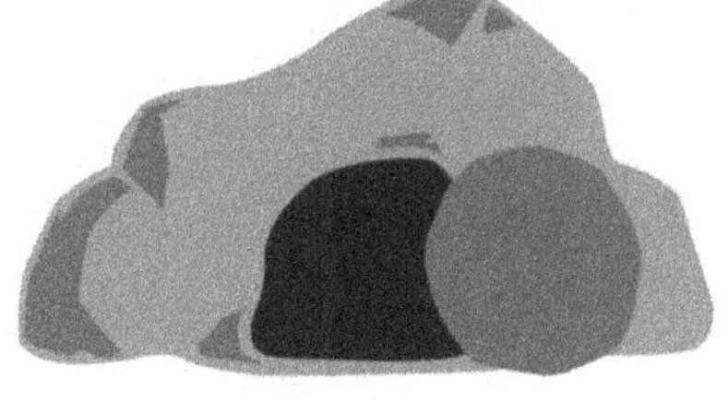

Just like God gave Jesus
a new, resurrected body,
God will one day give
all believers brand new,
perfect bodies to live
forever with Him (1 Corinthians 15:35–57).

Read these verses.

> *"Bodies made of flesh and blood can't share in the kingdom of God... And* ***we will be changed****. Our natural bodies don't last forever. They must be dressed with what does last forever. What dies must be dressed with* ***what does not die****."*
> 1 Corinthians 15:50, 52-54 (NIRV).

When we die, our bodies will be C __ __ __ __ __ __,

Our new bodies will never die.

So, there are three reasons why Jesus' resurrection is important.

1. The resurrection shows that Jesus is the Son of God, with the power to come back to life.
2. If Jesus had stayed dead, He would still be under the punishment and power of sin [death].
3. The resurrection shows that God will give believers a new body after they die.

Jesus' resurrection proved that He is God.
That's why it is so important!

5. What Happens to People Who Never Hear About JESUS?

The Bible tells us that believing in Jesus is the only way to be saved.

> *"Believe in the Lord Jesus, and you will be saved."*
> Acts 16:31 (NIV).

Only those who trust in Jesus will be forgiven and go to heaven.

So, what happens to people who never hear about Jesus?

What happens to people if they have never read the Bible?

The Bible tells us that God loves everyone and will make a way for everyone to learn about Him.

He does that by showing Himself to us in two different ways.

1. General Revelation

God shows Himself in Creation.

All you have to do is look around at the tall, snow-covered mountains and the powerful ocean waves.

Or watch a beautiful sunset or look carefully at the petals of a flower.

Our amazing world shows us that there is a Creator.

Read this Bible verse and fill in the blanks below.

> *"Ever since the world was created,* ***it has been possible to see the qualities of God that are not seen.*** *I'm talking about* ***His eternal power*** *and about the fact that He is God. Those things can be seen in what He has made. So, people have no excuse for what they do."*
> Romans 1:20 (NIRV).

This verse says that because of creation, it is possible to see the Q __ __ __ __ _ _ _ _ __ __ of God that cannot be seen with our eyes.

Because of creation,

We can see God's eternal P __ __ __ __.

We can know that He is G __ __.

So, people have N __ E __ __ __ __ __ for turning away from God.

Seeing God's power in creation gives everyone enough information to begin to know who God is.

God shows Himself in our Conscience.

God has given each person a conscience to know good and evil.

Everyone has a God-given moral compass.
We were born with an understanding of right and wrong.

Read this verse and fill in the blanks below.

> *"They show that what the law requires* ***is written on their hearts. The way their minds judge them*** *proves this fact. Sometimes,* ***their thoughts find them guilty.*** *At other times, their thoughts find them not guilty."*
> Romans 2:15 (NIRV).

God's L __ __ is written on our hearts.
His law tells us what is wrong and what is right.

Our M __ __ __ __ judge us.

Our T __ __ __ __ __ __ __ find us guilty.

When we do something wrong, we have that little voice in the back of our minds that tells us that we have sinned.

Oftentimes we feel guilty.

We know that what we did was wrong.
That is our conscience speaking to us.

God gave us a Spirit that wants to worship.

Missionaries often visit remote villages that have had no contact with the outside world.

They have not heard about God.
Yet, often, they find people worshipping man-made idols.

Even though they don't know anything about God, they still have the desire to worship something.

That's because God has given us a "spirit."

God has created us to have a personal relationship with Him.

We were created to worship God.

Everyone was created with the ability to know who God is when they look at creation.

We were all given a conscience and a spirit.

This is how God has shown us Himself in "general" revelation.

Everyone has some "general" understanding of God's existence.

So, those "who have never heard" have heard SOMETHING.

- They know that God exists.
- They know that there is a moral standard.
- They know that they have broken this standard.

It's not enough for salvation, but we can respond to what we DO know.

> *"But **they can't completely understand** what God has done from beginning to end."*
> Ecclesiastes 3:11 (NIRV).

If a person sees creation and wants to know who made it or if they realize that they have sinned because they have a guilty conscience, God will find a way for them to know more.

If a person truly desires to know God, God will find a way to make Himself known.

2. Special Revelation

General revelation teaches us that God exists and that there is right and wrong.

But we need more information if we are going to be saved.

People need to hear about Jesus.

Special Revelation is how God shows Himself to us through His Word, the Bible.

That is how we learn about Jesus.

Often times He will find someone who is willing to share the good news with them.

Read these verses and fill in the blanks.

> *"How, then, can they call on the one they have not believed in? And how can they believe in the one of whom they have not heard? And how can they hear without someone preaching to them?"*
> Romans 10:14-15 (NIV).

People cannot B __ __ __ __ __ __ in God until they hear the good news.

People cannot hear without a "P _ _ _ _ _ _ _ _."

If someone wants to know about God, He will send a messenger.

It doesn't have to be a church "preacher." Sometimes it will be a missionary.

Other times it might be a friend who cares enough to tell others.

Perhaps one day, you will be that messenger and tell others the good news of Jesus.

Our job is to make sure they hear.

God can use you to tell others about Jesus!

- Invite a friend to church with you,
- Give your neighbor a Bible.
- Share Jesus' love with your friends.

God doesn't want anyone to die without knowing Him.

He sends people to the right place at the right time so that those who are seeking Him WILL find Him.

"Those who have never heard" WILL have an opportunity to hear.

Everyone who truly seeks after God WILL find Him.

> *"You will find Him [God] if you seek Him with all your heart and with all your soul."*
> Deuteronomy 4:29 (NIRV).

Our loving God will always do what is right.

How Can Jesus Fit in My Heart?

You have probably heard that phrase before.

Someone might have encouraged you to pray and "ask Jesus into your heart" so that He will save you.

You might wonder, how will Jesus fit?

Did you know that the Bible doesn't say to ask Jesus into our hearts.

People say that as a way to try to explain how we get saved.

But it might actually make things more confusing.

Jesus doesn't want to come into our sinful hearts.
He wants to give us a brand NEW heart.

And He does that when we believe in Him.
When we trust Jesus to save us, God forgives our sins.

Keep reading to learn more about being saved.

Questions About People

1. Why Do People Get Sick and Die?

People get sick and die because of the evil that came into the world when Adam and Eve sinned.

God never wanted sickness and death.
When God created the world, everything in it was perfect.

In fact, the book of Genesis records the Creation and says, *"God saw that it was good."* Genesis 1:10 (NIV).

The world was perfect.
There was no sickness or disease.

So, what went wrong?

The Bible tells us that:

> ***"Sin entered the world because one man sinned.***
> ***And death came because of sin.***
> *Everyone sinned, so death came to all people."*
> Romans 5:12 (NIRV).

What entered the world? S __ __.

What came because of it? D __ __ __ __.

We are all sinners.

We choose to do the wrong thing all of the time.

And death is the result of sin.
Since we're all sinners, we will all die.

Ever since that day in the Garden of Eden, we've all had to live with the effects of sin entering into God's perfect creation.

So now, people get sick and die.

In fact, one day, we will all die physically.

But the great news is that we don't have to die spiritually.

If we have trusted in Jesus to save us, we will live forever.

2. If God Loves Me, Why Did My Dad Die?

As we learned in the last question, we live in a world where there are pain and death.

Unfortunately, even members of our family die.

There are many reasons why people die.

Sometimes people make bad choices.

- They might drink too much.
- They might drive too fast.

Sometimes, people get sick.

God allows sickness and death for several reasons.

- God gave us a free will – to choose right from wrong. We chose "wrong" and have to face the consequences.
- Pain and death can drive us to Jesus.

It's always sad when people die. Thankfully, God provided a way for us to be saved.

3. Why Do Some People Die When They Are Young?

When Adam and Eve chose to disobey God in the Garden of Eden, they were guilty of sin.

Read this Bible verse.

> *"**Sin entered the world because one man sinned.***
> *And death came because of sin.*
> *Everyone sinned, so death came to all people."*
> Romans 5:12 (NIRV).

Ever since, things have died.
Plants, animals, and people.

Death can come through accidents, sickness, or old age.

We must be ready because we never know what tomorrow might bring.

- When we are young, we often think that we are invincible.
- We often think that we have a long time to live.

But tomorrow is not promised to us.

The best news, though, is that if we have trusted in Jesus to save us, we will go immediately to heaven when we die.

God controls every breath we take, so we can trust He knows best.

If we have trusted in Jesus, death is not something to fear.

The big question is, if you were to die tonight, are you sure that you would go to be with Jesus in heaven?

If not – keep reading!

4. Do I Have to Love Everyone, Even Those Who Hate God?

God says in His Word that we should love and be kind to everyone.

- Even our enemies.
- Even God's enemies.

Sometimes, it can be hard always to be nice to everyone!

- Your little brother or sister, who you really do love, can sometimes be a real pain!
- Your best friend might say or do something that really irritates you.
- Strangers can be nasty, too!

But being nice to people is the right thing to do, especially as a Christian.

So, what does it mean to be nice?

- It might include acting in a polite, friendly or pleasant way.

- It might mean being considerate, and helpful.
- It means we speak kindly to others, even when they are unkind.

People who know Jesus have God's Spirit to help them do these things.

> *"But **the fruit of the Spirit** is love, joy, peace, forbearance, kindness, goodness, faithfulness, gentleness and self-control."*
> Galatians 5:22-23 (NIV).

What is the fifth fruit? K _ _ _ _ _ _ _ _.

- We are God's representatives.
- We are to show God's love to others.
- We might be the only way that someone learns about Jesus.

The Bible says:

> *"A new command I give you: **Love one another**. As I have loved you, so you must love one another."*
> John 13:34 (NIV).

What should we do to our enemies?

L _ _ _ O _ _ A _ _ _ _ _ _ _ _.

5. Is It Ever Okay to Punch Someone When They Are Mean?

This question is a bit like the last one.

Just because someone insulted you or said something rude or mean doesn't mean you have the right to hit them.

In fact, the Bible tells us to do the very opposite.

> *"But I tell you, do not resist an evil person.* ***If anyone slaps you on the right cheek, turn to them the other cheek****, also."*
> Matthew 5:39 (NIV).

If someone slaps you, what should you do back?

T___ T__ O_____ C_____.

If someone is mean to you, the Bible says to let them. Don't be mean back.

But what if they are hurting someone else?

In the Bible, all violence is wrong.

Read this verse.

> *"The Lord examines the righteous, but the wicked, those who love violence, He hates with a passion."*
> Psalm 11:5 (NIV).

God H _ _ _ _ violence.

Sometimes, showing love to others can turn things around.

Read this verse.

> *"Hatred stirs up conflict,*
> *but **love covers over all wrongs**."*
> Proverbs 10:12 (NIV).

What can love do?

C _ _ _ _ over all wrongs.

God will take care of the situation. Leave it up to Him.

Our job is to love others.

We can overcome evil with good.

Read these two verses and fill in the blanks below.

> *"Do not take revenge, my dear friends, but leave room for God's wrath, for it is written: "It is mine to avenge; I will repay," says the Lord.*
> *On the contrary: "**If your enemy is hungry, feed him; if he is thirsty, give him something to drink.** In doing this, you will heap burning coals on his head."*
> *Do not be overcome by evil,*
> *but **overcome evil with good.**"*
> Romans 12:19-20 (NIV).

We should not take R __ __ __ __ __ __.

God says, "I will R __ __ __ __."

Instead we should F __ __ __ our enemy.

We should give them something to D __ __ __ __.

That is how we overcome E __ __ __ with G __ __ __.

That is how we show God's love.

> *"Be **kind** and **compassionate** to one another, **forgiving** each other, just as in Christ God forgave you."*
> Ephesians 4:32 (NIV).

6. Why Doesn't My Dad Love Me Anymore?

Remember we talked about sin earlier in this book?

We all have a choice to do the right thing or to do wrong.

Parents also have a choice.
They are sinners just like you.
They can choose right or wrong, good or evil.

The sad thing is that our bad choices affect other people.

And nothing hurts more than when your dad (or mom) behaves like he doesn't love you.

I had a dad like that.

- He used to get really angry.
- He used to hit me.
- And then he left. He just walked out on us.

I don't know why he was like that, but I know that it wasn't my fault.

It was his choice to do the wrong thing.

Your dad might be mean to you or say horrible things.

If you have a dad or a mom like that, remember this.

You have a PERFECT Father.
He will never treat you badly.
He will never walk away.
God is the best Father ever!

God promises to be a father to the fatherless.

> *"**A Father to the fatherless**, a defender of widows, is God in His holy dwelling."*
> Psalm 68:5 (NIV).

God loves those who don't have a father at home, or those who have a father who treats people badly.

Our heavenly Father is the most perfect "Dad" there is!

If your earthly dad is not so great, look to your heavenly Dad!

He loves you more than you could ever imagine.

7. Why Does God Let Bad Things Happen?

Some questions are REALLY hard to answer.
This is one of them!

If God is love, then…

- Why did I get sick?
- Why did my friend die?
- Why did my parents get divorced?
- Why does God allow all of the evil, pain, and suffering in the world?

You might wonder:

- If God is as powerful as the Bible says, He could stop them all, couldn't He?
- If God is in control of everything, then He could fix it all, couldn't He?

Yes! God is all-powerful, all-wise, and all-good.

But sin changed everything.
Remember that we read about this before.

Sin introduced sickness, pain, and death into the world.

We are all sinners.
That means that…

- God allows us to make bad choices.
- God allows the consequences of sin to happen.

That's why bad things happen.

The good news is that one day, He will make everything right again.

In the meantime, we must trust in an ALL-POWERFUL God who loves us more than we could even imagine.

8. If God Is Always There, Why Didn't He Stop Me Getting Hurt?

This might be the hardest question yet!

We can be hurt in so many ways.

- We can get sick.
- We can be hurt in an accident.
- We can be hurt by other people.

Sometimes, it's the people who are supposed to love us that hurt us the most.

Some hurts are almost unspeakable.

Could God have stopped it?

Yes – He is all-powerful.

But He has given people a choice.

Unfortunately, people don't always make the right choice. And choices always have consequences.

My dad hurt me badly when I was a young teenager. My uncle hurt me, too.

It was difficult to recover from that abuse.

But I remembered how much God loved me and that really helped.

Here are some great verses from the Bible that will help.

> *"As a father has compassion on His children, so, the* ***Lord has compassion*** *on those who fear Him."*
> Psalm 103:13 (NIV).

God shows us C _ _ _ _ _ _ _ _ _.

> ***"The Lord is close to the brokenhearted*** *and* ***saves those who are crushed in spirit."***
> Psalm 34:18 (NIV).

God is C _ _ _ _ to us and S _ _ _ _ us.

God loves us more than we will ever know! Much more than our earthly friends and family.

God doesn't always stop the hurt, but He promises to be there with us.

Read these verses.

> *"Even though I walk through the darkest valley, I will fear no evil, **for You are with me**."*
> Psalm 23:4 (NIV).

> *"**Never will I leave you**; never will I forsake you."*
> Hebrews 13:5 (NIV).

God is always with us.

He will never L __ __ __ __ us or F __ __ __ __ __ __ __ us.

He will never hurt us or let us down.

When you don't understand why, trust your loving Father!

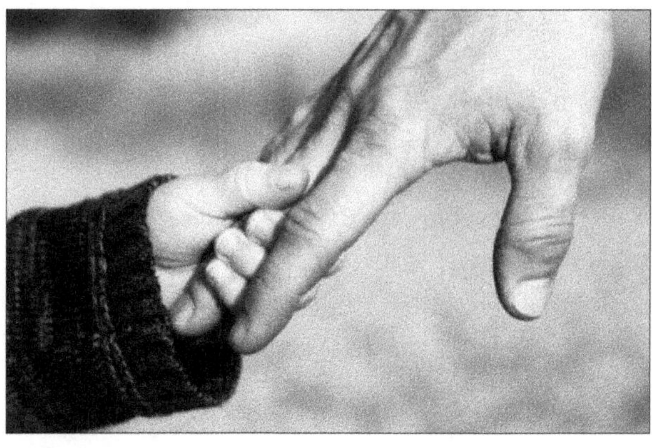

9. Are All Sins the Same with God?

Does God see all sins as equal?
Are they all the same?
Sin is sin, isn't it?

This is another hard question.

In one sense, yes.
All sin is the same in God's eyes.

- All sin separates us from God.
- All sin breaks our relationships with God.

Read this verse.

> *"For whoever keeps the whole law and yet stumbles at just one point is* ***guilty of breaking all of it.****"*
> James 2:10 (NIV).

This means that if we commited just one sin, God sees us as guilty of breaking the whole law.

His "law" is the "Ten Commandments."

You know them. Here are some of them.

- Honor thy father and mother.
- Thou shall not kill.
- Thou shall not commit adultery.
- Thou shall not steal.

So, this verse is telling us that if we commit one sin, it's the same as if we were to commit them all.

In this case, all sins are equal.

But in another sense, some sins are more serious. For example:

- Mass shooters at schools?
- Or people who abuse children?
- And surely, Adolf Hitler is the worst?

So, what makes some sins worse?

1. **The more we intend to sin, the more serious it is.**

   In other words, deciding to sin makes it worse.

   The Old Testament Law had lesser punishments for those who sinned unintentionally and greater punishments for those who sinned intentionally (defiantly). Read Numbers 15:27-31.

2. **The more serious the sin, the greater the consequences.**

> *"Do not be deceived: God cannot be mocked.*
> ***A man reaps what he sows."***
> Galatians 6:7 (NIV).

Different sins have different consequences.

- Stealing a cookie from the cookie jar might result in being hollered at.
- Bullying someone at school might get you suspended.
- Stealing an Xbox from the store might get you arrested.
- Killing someone will result in you going to prison.

3. **The more we know God, the more we are responsible to God.**

   Read this verse about Bible teachers.

> *"Not many of you should become teachers, my fellow believers, because you know that we who teach* ***will be judged more strictly.****"*
> James 3:1 (NIV).

Teachers have a big responsibility.
They must know the Bible and they must teach it accurately.

Therefore, people who teach others will be judged more S_ _ _ _ _ _ _ _.

Read this verse.

> *"From everyone who has been given much,* ***much will be demanded,*** *and from the one who has been entrusted with much, much more will be asked."*
> Luke 12:48 (NIV).

People who have been given more will be judged more.
The longer we know God, the more God expects from us.

So, yes, sin is sin!

Sin is equal in God's eyes.
But some sins will reap more serious **consequences** than others.

10. How Can God Forgive Murderers

Can God forgive murderers?
What about serial killers?

The answer is "yes."

But, let's be honest… there some sins seem unforgivable. And yet, God forgives.

Unfortunately, because of sin, horrible things happen in this world.

- God fully understands these unthinkable sins.
- Human life is sacred in God's eyes.
- Deliberately murdering someone is a terrible act.
- God hates what happened.
- God understands the pain it causes.

The fact that God might forgive such horrific crimes against innocent people is hard to understand.

Understanding God helps us understand why He forgives.

God is both merciful and just.

- God is merciful to those who ask for mercy.
- God is just and judges all sin.

Read this verse.

When Jesus died on the cross to pay our sin penalty, He paid for ALL sins.

> *"He [Jesus] gave His life to pay for our sins.*
> *But He not only paid for our sins.*
> ***He also paid for the sins of the whole world."***
> 1 John 2:2 (NIRV).

When Jesus died on the cross, He paid for the sins of the W __ __ __ __ world.

- He forgives the "little" sins, like lying, being angry, or thinking bad thoughts.
- He forgives the "big" ones, like kidnapping and murder.

Jesus will forgive any and every sin.

That includes past, present, and future, big or small.

A murderer will, no doubt, face serious consequences like losing family and friends and spending time in prison.

But his sins will be completely forgiven when he trusts in Jesus for salvation.

Never forget:

NONE of us DESERVES God's forgiveness and salvation.

> *"Because of what the Son [Jesus] has done, we have been set free. Because of Him,* ***all our sins have been forgiven.****"*
> Colossians 1:14 (NIRV).

We have been set free because of what J _ _ _ _ has done for us.

We have been F _ _ _ _ _ _ _ because of Jesus.

Remember:
It is not the size of the sin that matters.
It's the size of Jesus' sacrifice.

11. What If Someone in My Family Doesn't Believe in God?

Family is important!

Family helps to shape important things in our lives, like attitudes, habits, and beliefs.

Sometimes, though, members of our family might believe things which go against what the Bible teaches.

So, what do we do if someone we love doesn't believe in God?

What if they think differently?

It might be your mom or dad or a brother or sister.

The Bible gives us some good answers to help in this situation.

1. Honor Them

If it's your parents, the Bible tells us always to honor them, even if they don't believe in God.

Read this verse.

> ***"Honor your father and your mother."***
> Exodus 20:12 (NIV).

We don't use the word "honor" much any more.
Do you know what it means to honor someone?

- Honoring someone means to show them value, respect, and support.
- It means recognizing their role in giving you life, and that they are significant.
- It means that you are polite and respectful, even if the relationship is difficult.

Listen to your parents and respect them.

> *"Children, **obey your parents** in the Lord, for this is right."*
> Ephesians 6:1 (NIV).

Tell them how much you love them, and show it by living a life that pleases God.

2. Live like Jesus.

Don’t preach at them.
Don't correct them.

Just live the way that God wants you to live.

> *"Be wise in the way you act toward outsiders; make the most of every opportunity.* ***Let your conversation be always full of grace.***"
> Colossians 4:5-6 (NIV).

If an opportunity comes to share your faith, do it with love and respect.

3. Pray for Them.

God can change your parent's hearts.
He can show them the truth.

Pray that all of your family will trust Him too.
Never give up.

12. Why Did My Parents Get Divorced?

God created marriage (Genesis 2:24), but He didn't create divorce.

God created marriage to be permanent, but sometimes people make sinful choices that lead to divorce.

There are many reasons why they might choose to end their marriage.

Sometimes it's a result of sin.
Sometimes it is in reponse to sin.

Either way, divorce is a very hard thing for everybody involved, especially the children.

If your parents are choosing divorce, you may be feeling sad, angry, or afraid.

God understands the hurt you're going through.

Remember:
God loves you and will take care of you.

Read this verse.

> *"Turn all your worries over to Him.* ***He cares about you.****"*
> 1 Peter 5:7 (NIRV).

God tells us to give Him your W _ _ _ _ _ _ _.

Why?

Because God C _ _ _ _ about you.

Remember:

Your parents' divorce is not your fault!

Whatever bad choices your parents made that led them to choose to end their marriage, they had nothing to do with you.

You did not somehow cause this to happen, so don't blame yourself.

13. What Does God Think About War?

The Bible says that all violence is wrong.

> *"The Lord examines the righteous, but the wicked, those who love violence,* ***He hates with a passion.****"*
> Psalm 11:5 (NIV).

- God hates violence.
- God hates fighting.
- God hates war.

Life is precious.
God hate anything that puts life in danger.

So why doesn't God stop war?

We already talked about how God is all-powerful.

- He could stop wars if He wanted.
- He could stop anything.
- He could force people to stop fighting.
- He could even force us to love Him.

God gave people a free will and a choice but that would make us robots.

God doesn't want robots.
He wants us to choose Him.

But many people choose evil.
So, for now, God allows war.

But one day, there will be no more violence, fighting or war.

> *"**He will wipe every tear** from their eyes. There will be **no more death or mourning or crying or pain.**"*
> Revelation 21:4 (NIV).

14. Why Is Sex Outside of Marriage Wrong?

Does God want to spoil our fun, or is there another reason?

God, in His wisdom, designed sex to be sacred and holy, for married couples to enjoy.

God designed sex so that married couples could have a family.

He told Adam and Eve,

> *"God blessed them [Adam and Eve]. He said, "**Have little ones** so that there will be many of you."*
> Genesis 1:22 (NIRV).

God wanted them to have children.

God created sex for people, **who are married**, but whatever God creates, Satan works to destroy.

Having sex outside of marriage creates all sorts of problems.

The Bible says:

> ***"But the body is not meant for sexual sins...***
> *Keep far away from sexual sins."*
> 1 Corinthians 6:13, 18 (NIRV).

God knows what is best for us.

His design is for us to wait until we are married.

Questions About My Relationship with God

1. How Do I Get to Heaven?

Do you get gifts at Christmas or on your birthday?

Imagine if a friend gave you a special gift. How would you feel if, after you open it, they asked you to pay for it?

Would it be a gift if you had to pay for it?

> *"For it is by grace you have been saved, through faith - and this is not from yourselves,* ***it is the gift of God.****"*
> Ephesians 2:8 (NIV).

Of course not.

Heaven is a gift.

It doesn't cost you anything (Jesus paid the price!).
Nor can you pay for it.
If you could, Jesus wouldn't have had to die!

It is impossible to earn our way to heaven.
Nothing you DO can get you to heaven.
Jesus did it ALL!

2. What Does it Mean to Believe in Jesus?

We already talked about sin and its penalty.
We are all sinners deserving of death.

The Bible says that we can be saved through faith.
Faith is another word for "trust" or "belief."

Read this verse.

> *"For God so loved the world that He gave His only Son, that* ***whoever BELIEVES in Him will not perish****, but have eternal life."*
> John 3:16 (NIV).

What must we do to have eternal life? B _ _ _ _ _ _.

"Believe" is another word for "trust."

- When you sat down today, did you check the chair legs to make sure they weren't broken?
- Did you make sure all of the screws and nails were tight?

- Do you check that the back of the chair is firmly attached?

Most people just sit down.
They are trusting (or believing) that the chair will hold them up.

Just as you trust (or believe) that a chair will hold you up through no effort of your own when you sit on it, you must trust Jesus Christ to get you to heaven through no effort of your own.

People sometimes are confused by what it means to believe.

Believing is not hard. It's not something you DO.

If I asked you, "What is the object in this picture?"
What would you say?

"It's a pen!"

Imagine if I said, "No. That's too easy.
You need to believe harder."

That doesn't make sense, does it?
Believing is just believing.

If you believe it is a pen, you don't need to believe "harder" or do something extra to help you believe.

If you are convinced that it is a pen, then you believe.

The great news is that God promises that whoever BELIEVES in Him has eternal life.

Read this verse.

> *"Whoever hears my Word and **believes** in Him who sent Me HAS eternal life."*
> John 5:24.

If we believe that Jesus paid our sin penalty, the Bible tells us that we will be saved.

We just need to believe God's promise

We must trust in Jesus Christ ALONE, and God will give US eternal life as a FREE gift!

3. Can I Get to Heaven by Being Good?

Can our good works get us to heaven?

Some people think that if their good works outweigh the bad, then God will let them into heaven.

So, they spend their lives trying to be "good."

- They try to obey their parents.
- They go to church.
- They pray.
- Some even get baptized.

But there is a problem.

The Bible says:

> *"All of us have become like one who is unclean, and **all our righteous acts are like filthy rags**."*
> Isaiah 64:5-6 (NIV).

God sees our good works ("righteous acts") just the same as F __ __ __ __ __ R __ __ __.

No one likes dirty rags. They smell bad and can be slimy and gross.

If we think that we can get into heaven by good works, we will be out of luck.

God doesn't want them.

That means,

- Going to church won't help pay the cost.
- Praying won't help pay the cost.
- Giving money to the poor won't help pay the cost.
- Being baptized doesn't clean you.

God doesn't want our good works.

Read this verse:

> *"But things are different with God. He makes ungodly people right with Himself. If people* ***trust*** *[believe] in Him, their faith is accepted* ***even though they do not work****. Their* ***faith*** *makes them right with God."*
> Romans 4:5 (NIV).

The Bible says that our F __ __ __ __ is accepted, when we

D __ N__ __ W __ __ __.

We can't pay our sin penalty with good works.
Trying to work our way to heaven is not possible.
Our "faith" is our entry ticket, not our works.

If we could get into heaven by our good works, then Jesus didn't need to die.

We just accept God's free gift.

When someone gives you a gift,
do you pay them for it?

No!

It's a gift.
It's free.

It is no longer a gift if we try to pay for it.

God sent His Son to die on the cross so that we wouldn't have to. It was a very special FREE GIFT.

We just simply believe that when Jesus died on the cross for our sins.

No "good" works required!
Jesus did it all.
THAT'S GREAT NEWS!

4. Can I be Sure I Will Go to Heaven?

It's a great question.
Can we know FOR SURE that we will go to heaven?

The Bible says, "YES!"

You can be sure.

Why? Because God promised.
He said that if you believe in Jesus, you WILL be saved!
And God ALWAYS keeps His promises.

The Bible says:

> *"Very truly, I tell you, whoever hears My word and believes Him who sent Me **HAS** eternal life and will not be judged but has crossed over from death to life."*
> John 5:24 (NIV).

Once we believe in Jesus, our sins are forgiven, and we can know for sure that we will go to Heaven one day to be with Him.

5. I've Trusted in Jesus. Now What?

After we trust in Jesus to save us, God wants us to learn more about Him.

God wants us to become "disciples."
A disciple is a learner and a follower.

How do we become a "disciple" of Jesus?

1. Read the Bible.

When we first trust in Jesus, the Bible says that we are "baby" Christians.

You are in the "baby" stage, and just like babies, you need "milk" to grow!

> *"Like newborn babies, **crave pure spiritual milk**, so that by it you may grow in your salvation."*
> 1 Peter 2:2 (NIV).

"Spiritual milk" is talking about the Bible.

Reading the Bible is a way for us to hear from God.

It is God's way of speaking to us, and telling us how to live well.

- Reading the Bible teaches us how to be more like Jesus.
- Reading the Bible helps us to sin less.

> *"I have **hidden Your Word in my heart** that I might not sin against You."*
> Psalm 119:11 (NIV).

When we read God's Word, we will learn and grow to become more like Jesus.

2. Pray.

Reading the Bible is how God talks to us.
Prayer is how we talk to God.

You don't need to say any special words.

Just talk to Him the same way that you talk to your friend.

God wants to hear how you're feeling, so just be honest.

When you spend some time each day reading the Bible and praying, you will be able to grow closer to Him and become more like Jesus.

3. Go to church.

Just like we get together with family and friends, we also need to go to church.

It is awesome that we can talk to God anytime and anywhere.

But God wants us to encourage each other as well.

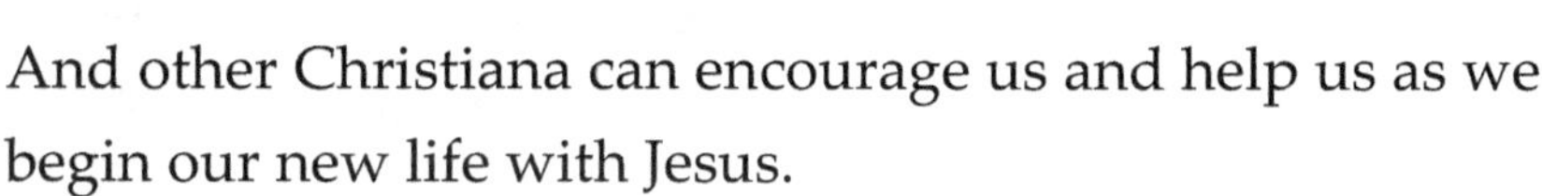

And other Christiana can encourage us and help us as we begin our new life with Jesus.
We need each other.

Read this verse.

> *"And **let us not give up meeting together**. Some are in the habit of doing this. Instead, let us encourage one another with words of hope."*
> Hebrews 10:25 (NIRV).

Going to church each week should be a H __ __ __ __.

Going to church should be a regular practice, not one that you need to decide about each week.

- "Should we go to church this morning?"
- "I'm tired, so I might stay home."
- "We were invited to go to the beach with our friends this Sunday. Beach or church? Which one should we choose?

Church shouldn't be a decision that you make each week. It should be a habit.

Find someone that you know loves Jesus (besides your parent); maybe a Sunday School teacher or a friend from church.

See if they might be willing to meet with you each week or so to encourage you and help you to grow.

Now that you have trusted in Jesus, God wants you to grow.

Babies don't stay babies.
They grow.

Each of these things will help you grow to become more like Jesus.

7. Why Should I Pray If God Already Knows What Will Happen?

If God's plan always happens, why should we pray and ask God for things?

The Bible says that God has already planned what will happen.

> *"The Lord who rules over all has made a promise. He has said, "**You can be sure that what I have planned will happen**. What I have decided will take place."*
> Isaiah 14:24 (NIRV).

God promises that His plans WILL happen!
So why pray?

1. God tells us to pray.

> ***"Never stop praying."***
> 1 Thessalonians 5:17 (NIRV).

If we don't pray, God will still carry out His plan, but we will not have been a part of His work or learned to know Him more.

God works out His perfect plan through prayer.

But when we pray, we are obeying God's command and following His example.

2. Jesus taught us to pray.

You might recognize these verses. It called the Lord's Prayer.

> ***"This is how you should pray.***
> *'Our Father in heaven, hallowed be Your name. May Your kingdom come. May Your will be done on earth as it is in heaven. Give us this day our daily bread. And forgive us our sins, just as we have forgiven those who sin against us."*
> Matthew 6:9-12 (NIRV).

Some call it "the disciple's prayer" because it shows US (not the Lord) how to pray.

We should pray that God's name will be

H _ _ _ _ _ _ _.

God's name is special and we should treat it that way.

We should not swear or use God's name to curse.

We should pray that God's kingdom will come and that His will would be done on earth.

- We should be praying that God's rule and perfect will be done here on Earth, just as it is in Heaven.
- We should be praying that God's peace and order will come to the world.
- We should pray for God to provide for our daily needs.
- And we should pray for God's forgiveness.

We might have trusted in Jesus to save us, but we still sin each day.

3. Jesus prayed.

Before Jesus was arrested, He prayed that God might take away His suffering.

Can you imagine knowing that you were about to be crucified.

Jesus knew the pain He was about to face, and He prayed that it would be taken away.

Read this verse.

> *"Then He [Jesus] fell with His face to the ground. He prayed, "My Father,* ***if it is possible, take this cup of suffering away from Me.*** *But let what You want be done, not what I want."*
> Matthew 26:39 (NIRV).

Even though He didn't want to die, Jesus obeyed.
He did what God wanted.

We should also pray for God's will, even though it might not be pleasant.

8. Can Christians Lose Their Salvation?

This is a great question.
Many people wonder about this, and you will probably meet people who will disagree.

But the Bible teaches that once we are saved, we cannot be "unsaved."

Let's take a closer look.

When we trust in Jesus to save us, we become a member of God's forever family. The Bible says that we are "born" into His family.

Read these verses.

> *"Jesus replied, "Very truly I tell you, no one can see the kingdom of God **unless they are born again**."*
> John 3:3 (NIV).

> *"Yet to all who did receive Him [Jesus], to those who believed in His name, He gave the right to become **children of God**."*
> *John 1:12 (NIV).*

Jesus said that we must be B _ _ _ again.

When we believe in His name, we become

C _ _ _ _ _ _ _ _ of God.

We are a part of God's forever family.

Once you are born into a family, you cannot be "unborn." No matter what you do, your parents will always be your parents.

Even if you do something really bad, and they:

- Throw you out of the home.
- Never speak to you again.
- Leave you zero inheritance.

But you are still their child.

Some people still think that God can throw them out of the family, but look at these verses.

> *"My sheep listen to My voice; I know them, and they follow Me. I give them eternal life, and they shall never perish;* ***no one will snatch them out of My hand.****"*
> John 10:27-29 (NIV).

God holds you in the palm of His H _ _ _.

No one can S _ _ _ _ _ us out.

Read these verses.

Nothing can separate you from God's love.

> *"For I am convinced that* ***neither death nor life, neither angels nor demons, neither the present nor the future, nor any powers, neither height nor depth nor anything else in all creation,*** *will be able to separate us from the love of God that is in Christ Jesus our Lord."*
> Romans 8:38-39 (NIV).

What things cannot separate us fom God's love?

Not D _ _ _ _ or L _ _ _.

Not A _ _ _ _ _ or D _ _ _ _ _.

Not the P _ _ _ _ _ _ or the F _ _ _ _ _.

Not any P _ _ _ _ _.

Not H _ _ _ _ _ or D _ _ _ _

Not A _ _ _ _ _ _ _ in all C _ _ _ _ _ _ _.

I think that pretty much covers everything, don't you?

But what if we disobey God?

When we disobey, there will be consequences (just like in your human family).

But that doesn't mean that you are thrown out of the family. That is not possible!

What if we don't believe anymore?
That doesn't change God's love for you.

What if we don't want to be in God's family anymore?

Can we leave our human family?

- You can move out of the family home.
- You can decide to never speak to your family again.
- You can choose to never see them again.

But you are still part of the family.
You cannot be "unborn."
Your parents will always be your parents.

So, can you lose your salvation?
Can you be "un-born"?

The anwer is "no."

For more answers, see "Understanding Salvation" by the same author.

Other Questions

1. What Happened to the Dinosaurs?

The Bible doesn't directly mention dinosaurs, so we don't know for sure.

According to the Bible, the dinosaurs were created along with the other land animals.

People were created on the same day, so dinosaurs lived at the same time.

Read these verses.

> *"And God said, "Let the land produce living creatures according to their kinds: the livestock,* ***the creatures that move along the ground, and the wild animals,*** *each according to its kind." And it was so."*
> Genesis 1:24 (NIV).

God created everything.

> *"Through Him [God] all things were made."*
> John 1:3 (NIV).

The Bible also says that God created the "Behemoth."

> ***"Look at Behemoth,*** *which I made along with You and which feeds on grass like an ox."*
> Job 40:15-19 (NIV).

According to the dictionary, "behemoths" are enormous or “monstrous” creatures.

Behemoths are probably dinosaurs.

So, what happened to them?

Some Bible experts believe dinosaurs died out before the great flood.

Others believe they went aboard the ark with the rest of the animals. The rest died in the flood and became fossils.

Others believe they went aboard the ark with the rest of the animals.

Of course, nobody whether they did or not because we weren’t around, and the Bible doesn’t tell us.

But if they went on the ark like the other animals, at least two of each kind would have survived along with Noah and his family. The rest died in the flood and became fossils.

What would have happened to the ones who survived?

- The flood caused changes to the climate.
- There would have been a lack of food until crops were planted and harvested.
- Disease was a part of life and might have wiped them out.
- And man's activities no doubt caused many types of animals to become extinct.

The dinosaurs, like many other creatures, eventually died out.

Again, we don't know for sure because we weren't there.

2. Who Did Cain Marry?

Many people wonder, "If Adam and eve were the only people on earth, who did Cain marry?

Again, the Bible doesn't tell us.

We know that after God created Adam and Eve, they had sons and daughters (Genesis 5:4).

"After Seth was born, Adam lived 800 years and had other sons and daughters."
Genesis 5:4 (NIV).

Some people think that Cain married his sister because he had no one else to marry.

Others think that maybe God created other people after Adam and Eve, so Cain might have married one of them.

But these are just guesses because the Bible doesn't tell us.

We can ask God when we get to heaven!

3. Did Adam Have a Belly Button?

We are not told if Adam had a belly button, but the answer is probably "no."

Belly buttons are formed when the doctor cuts the cord from our moms after we are born.

Adam was not "born" like we were.
He was "created."

Adam did not have a mom.
So, chances are that he didn't have a belly button.

God could have created him with one, but there wouldn't have been a reason to.

It's another answer that we will have to wait for.
When we get to heaven we can ask.

4. Did God Create Other Universes or Just This One?

God created everything!

> *"In the beginning God created the **heavens** and the **earth**."*
> Genesis 1:1 (NIV).

God created the world we live in.

He also created the heavens. The sun, moon, stars, and other planets.

But are there other universes?

We can only see so far.
Our telescopes are not able to see beyond our galaxy.

The Bible does not tell us if there is anything beyond.

The Bible doesn't tell us whether there are other people out in space.

So, anything people tell you is just a guess.

Somehow, I think that if God wanted us to know, He would have told us.

5. Are There Really More Than Two Genders?

The world is telling us that there are many genders.
You have probably seen and heard people who believe in many different "genders."

"You can be whatever you want."
"You can be whatever you feel."

This confusion has been around since Bible times, so it's not a new question.

The difference is that this issue used to be hidden.

- Now, it's out in the open.
- Now, it's in our faces 24/7 on the news and social media.
- Now, it is accepted.
- Now, you are bullied or even arrested if you disagree.

It's easy to be pulled into our world.
It's easy to go along with the crowd and believe what they are telling you.

But don't be fooled by what you read and see out there.

- Just because it is online doesn't make it true.
- Just because it's taught at school doesn't mean it's true.

The Bible says:
God created Adam and Eve. MALE and FEMALE.

> *"So, God created mankind in His own image, in the image of God He created them;* ***male and female*** *He created them."*
> Genesis 1:26-27 (NIV).

God made people M __ __ __ and F __ __ __ __ __ __.

Only TWO genders.

Regardless of what you hear from the world, your sex (or gender) was established before you were born.

My daughter found out from a blood test that she was having twin boys.

Their gender was not "assigned" at birth.
They were boys before they were born. It was in their DNA.

So no, there are not more than two genders.
There are not 78 or 15.

There are just TWO!
Male and female.

That is not a very popular opinion today.
But it's the truth.
God's truth!

Do your own research. Read the only real TRUTH – the Bible.

6. What Do Rainbows Really Mean?

The rainbow was created to be God's sacred symbol of His covenant with man.

The rainbow was placed in the sky after the flood. The rainbow represents God's promise to never again destroy the world with a flood (Genesis 9:12-17).

Unfortunately, our understanding of a rainbow has been twisted by a "flag."

The "Rainbow Flag" was designed in 1977 to symbolize the gay pride movement.

It is a global symbol of LGBTQ+ pride.

It's supposed to represent the different views of human sexuality and gender.

It's supposed to represent acceptance.

It's supposed to represent hope and healing.

However:

- The rainbow is NOT a sign of God's forgiveness and acceptance.

- It is NOT a sign of the unity between man and God.
- It is NOT a sign of the end of God's anger.

It is a sign to the world that we should remember God's covenant to never flood the earth again.

God is **holding back** His anger.
God is still angry with sin and sinners.
He does not accept our "different views of sexuality and gender."

Unfortunately, when we see a rainbow on a flag or a t-shirt now, we tend to think of man's warped ideas, not God's promise.

Remember: The rainbow is about God and His promise!

For more answers about "gender," see "Understanding Me," by the same author.

Congratulations

You have completed "UNDERSTANDING HARD QUESTIONS."

Write your name and date on your certificate, and have your parent or a teacher sign it for you.

Note To Parents

Most parents want to do the right thing, but so often, they are either too busy or overwhelmed. You need to be a good role model to set an example for your children. They are watching.

Here are some suggestions to get you started.

- Make sure your children have a Bible of their own. Make sure it's age-appropriate. They can't read it if they don't understand it (see the following page recommendations).

- Provide notebooks for each child to write down what they learn. Encourage them to write down their prayer requests and the answers to their prayers.

- Encourage them to read their Bible for five minutes every day. We suggest that you begin with the book of John.

- Encourage them to write down any questions and ask you or their Sunday School teacher.

- Make time each day to read your own Bible. Kids learn by watching you. Set a good example for them to follow.

Choosing The Best Bible for Your Child

Here are some recommendations for Bibles to help your kids get excited about God's Word!

MAKE AN AGE-APPROPRIATE CHOICE.

If you want your children to enjoy reading the Bible, buy one that is easy to read, attractive, and engaging. Too often, kids struggle to look up verses at church in a Bible that has tiny print, is in a hard-to-read translation, and has no pictures or illustrations to draw them in.

Paul wrote to young Timothy,

> "And how **from childhood** you have been acquainted with the sacred writings, which are able to make you wise for salvation through faith in Christ Jesus."
> 2 Timothy 3:15 (NIV).

Timothy began studying the Bible as a young child. As parents, we want our kids to know and love God's Word, so buy them a Bible that they will understand.

BUY A BIBLE FOR EACH CHILD

Each child needs their own copy of the Bible. As parents, we spare no expense to buy our kids whatever they need to succeed in school or sports. Do the same for God's Word. Buy them a Bible that they will love to read.

The New International Version for Young Readers (NIrV), the New International Version (NIV), or the English Standard Version (ESV) are good translations for kids.

It's one of the most important investments you can make in your child's Christian education and spiritual development.

RECOMMENDED BIBLES FOR CHILDREN

Here are some examples of recommended Bibles available today.

PRESCHOOL

My Awesome God Storybook

The MY AWESOME GOD Storybook Bible is ideal for parents who want to read the key stories of the Bible to their young children. This Bible includes a topical index and helpful discussion questions.

YOUNGER ELEMENTARY

NIrV Adventure Bible for Early Readers – For Ages 5–10

This is a simpler version of the children's NIV Bible created for younger readers.

One of the easiest translations is the New International Reader's Version (NIrV). The NIrV is the young reader's edition of this fun, interactive Bible that helps children learn about what they are reading through helpful information presented throughout.

NIV Adventure Bible – For Ages 8–11

The bestselling NIV Adventure Bible® will get kids excited about reading the Scriptures! Your kids will be captivated by the full-color features that make it fun and engaging to read the Bible and memorize their favorite verses.

CSB Explorer Bible
This Bible reads similarly to the NCV translation and is filled with fun activities, maps, and images that your kids will not want to put down.

UPPER ELEMENTARY
Your preteen children can really start to master the Word of God! Here are some exciting options!

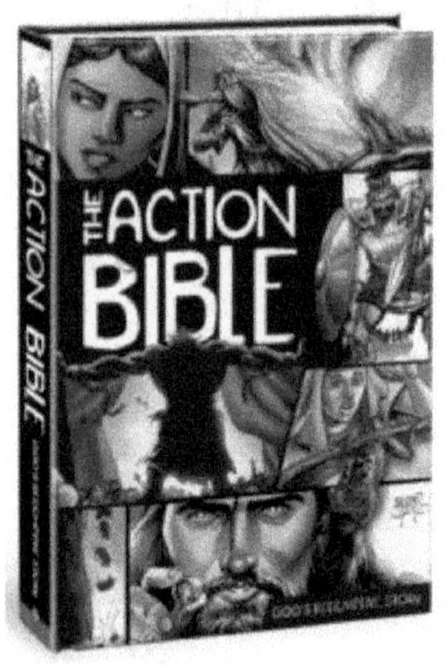

The Action Bible
The Action Bible presents the entire Bible in cool comic book illustrations. Kids will read it cover to cover many times over.

The Action Bible Study Bible
The creators of the Action Comic Bible also published a Study Bible edition in both the NIV and ESV.

The Action Study Bible is the complete text of the Bible, with select illustrations from the Action Bible throughout.

The Understanding Life Series.

UNDERSTANDING SALVATION is a short workbook designed for children ages 7-12 to use independently or with a parent.

It presents the good news of Jesus in a clear and easy-to-understand way that will help them know FOR SURE that they will live with Jesus in heaven one day.

Children will learn the key principles of salvation, teaching the "Bad News" (sin) and "Good News" (Jesus), along with Bible verses and simple illustrations.

This 120-page book will help them deepen their understanding of God's grace and begin their relationship with Him.

UNDERSTANDING BAPTISM is a 95-page workbook designed for children ages 8-12 to use independently or with a parent or leader.

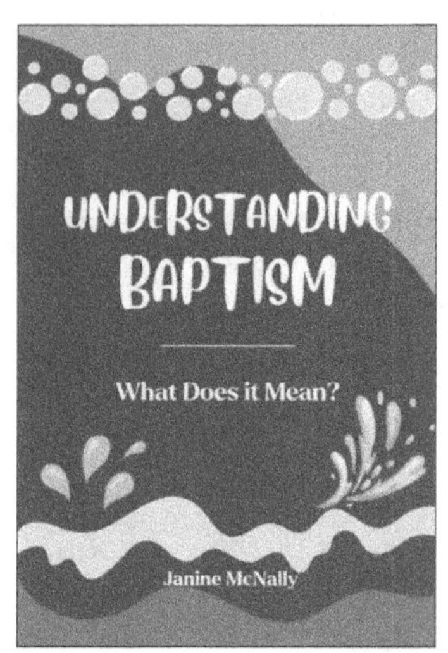

It is intended for those who have already expressed their belief in Jesus for salvation and have asked about being baptized.

This book answers these questions.

- How can we be saved?
- Can I be sure I am saved?
- What is baptism?
- Why should I be baptized?
- When should I be baptized?
- What happens during a baptism?

UNDERSTANDING GOD is the third book in the "Understanding Life" series for Kids, written for children ages 9-12.

Children are asking questions every day about God, the Bible, salvation, life, death, the afterlife, angels, demons, and more.

We need to be prepared with answers, or they will look elsewhere.

This 135-page book answers the following questions.

1. What is God like?
2. How did He create the world?
3. Who Created God?
4. Who is the Holy Spirit?
5. How can Jesus be God but also be God's Son?
6. Why does God let bad things happen?
7. Can God make mistakes?
8. Does God Love Me?

This book can be used as a training resource for your volunteers or as a parent.

UNDERSTANDING the BIBLE is the fourth book in the series.

When your child asks the tough questions, do you have answers for them? Do they know how to read the Bible and apply it in their lives?

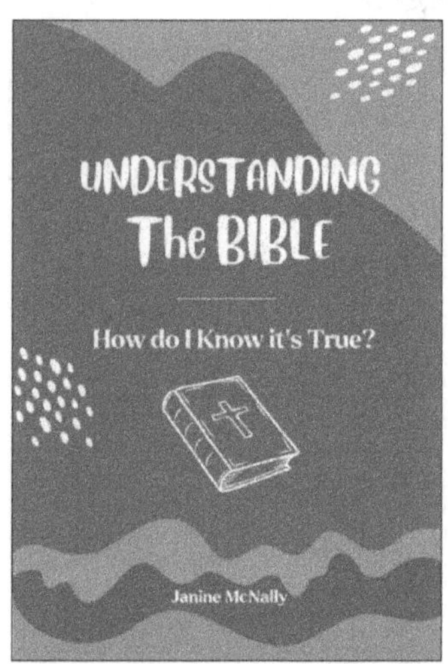

- How do we know the Bible is true?
- Is the Bible trustworthy?
- How do we know that it is really God's Word?

Written for children ages 8-12, this 120-page book teaches some basic Bible apologetics.

The content includes:
Three Big Words:

1. Inspiration - Written by God and Man
2. Inerrancy - No mistakes
3. Preservation

The Bible's Structure
How to Have a Quiet Time
How to Memorize God's Word

UNDERSTANDING ME addresses the big question, "Who am I?" in this 120-page book for kids ages 9-12.

Our world says, "There's no right or wrong," "We decide what is true and right," and "We can create our own identity."

At a time when kids are going through enormous changes, they are confronted with ambiguity and confusion.

1. Who am I?
2. Am I loved?
3. Am I alone?
4. Why am I here?

Each question is handled from a Biblical perspective and ends with the hope of a new life, a new body, and a new world for those who have trusted in Jesus.

UNDERSTANDING HARD QUESTIONS is the sixth book in the "Understanding Life" series for kids.

It answers 56 of the most common questions asked by kids from a Biblical perspective and in an age-appropriate way.

- Who created God?
- Does God speak to people?
- Will God stop loving me if I keep sinning?
- How did Jesus perform miracles?
- Why do people get sick and die?
- Why did my parents get divorced?
- Can Christians lose their salvation?
- How can God forgive murderers?
- Why is sex outside of marriage wrong?
- Are there more than two genders?
- Can I be sure that I will go to heaven?

Written for kids ages 9-12, this 165-page book answers these questions using basic Bible apologetics.

UNDERSTANDING LIFE & DEATH is written for children ages 8-12 and addresses the questions that arise when a child experiences the death of a loved one.

- Why Do People Get Sick and Die?
- What Happens After You Die?
- If God Loves Me, Why Did My Dad Die?
- What is Heaven Like?
- Will Everyone Go to Heaven No Matter What They Believe?
- Do People Who Never Hear About Jesus Go to Heaven?
- Is Hell Real?
- How Could a Loving God Send People to Hell?
- Why Did God Create Satan?

This 120-page book answers these questions and more from a Biblical perspective in an age-appropriate way. It aims to provide help and hope in times of sadness and grief.

About the Author

Originally a high school teacher in her native Australia, Janine McNally has partnered with her husband for many years of pastoral ministry.

Janine graduated with a Master of Theology from Dallas Theological Seminary and a Doctor of Ministry from Grace School of Theology.

She is the author of "When You See Fireflies—Equipping Leaders and Parents to Minister Effectively to Generation Alpha," the "Understanding Life for Kids" series, seven devotional books for kids ("10 Minutes with God"), and "STEPS to Knowing Jesus" for kids and preteens.

She passionately believes in reaching kids for Jesus and enlightening leaders and parents about Generation Alpha and beyond.

Janine and Gary have been married for thirty-two years and live in Panama City, Florida.

They have three grown children, Hannah (married to Kevin), Jonathan (married to Brayton), and Jami Grace.

They also have three beautiful grandchildren, Grayson, Hunter, and Emerson.

About the Ministry

Janine McNally directs the operations of **Equipping Fireflies**, a non-profit dedicated to providing gospel-centered resources that proclaim a message that will grab the attention of this generation, break the magnetic attraction of the increasingly dark world, and lead children to the Light.

THE STORY BEHIND THE NAME

> "When do we have to come inside?"
> "When you see the fireflies."

Our kids loved to play outside, but as night began to fall, it was time to come in, where it was safe. Each evening, for a short time, the fireflies would light up our entire backyard. Their unmistakable glow was the signal that it was time.

Our world has become much darker. We desperately need the kids and their families to hear the call. "Come inside where it's safe." The world is rapidly becoming bleaker as the generations race by, yet our children are running towards the night.

We must proclaim a message that grabs their attention, one that they understand and that will break the magnetic attraction of the increasingly dark world.

*"**You are the light of the world.***
***Let your light shine** before others that they may see your good deeds and glorify your Father in heaven."*
Matthew 5:14; 16

OUR PASSION
Statistics show that most Christians trusted Christ between the ages of 3 and 12. Our passion is to reach children for Jesus and serve, equip, and encourage Children's Ministry leaders and parents.

THE GOOD NEWS
When Jesus died on the cross, He did EVERYTHING that God requires for us to go to heaven when we die."

Lighting the Way for the Next Generations.
www.equippingfireflies.com

"And these words which I command you today shall be in your heart. You shall teach them diligently to your children, and shall talk of them when you sit in your house, when you walk by the way, when you lie down, and when you rise up.
You shall bind them as a sign on your hand, and they shall be as frontlets between your eyes. You shall write them on the doorposts of your house and on your gates."
Deuteronomy 6:6-9

www.ingramcontent.com/pod-product-compliance
Lightning Source LLC
Chambersburg PA
CBHW061723020426
42331CB00006B/1065

* 9 7 9 8 9 8 9 6 7 3 2 8 5 *